THE UNEXPLAINED

GHOSTS

BY ADAM STONE

BELLWETHER MEDIA · MINNEAPOLIS MN

TM

Are you ready to take it to the extreme?
Torque books thrust you into the action-packed world
of sports, vehicles, mystery, and adventure. These books
may include dirt, smoke, fire, and dangerous stunts.
WARNING: read at your own risk.

Library of Congress Cataloging-in-Publication Data

Stone, Adam.
 Ghosts / by Adam Stone.
     p. cm. -- (Torque: The unexplained)
Summary: "Engaging images accompany information about ghosts. The combination of high-interest subject matter and light text is intended for students in grades 3 through 7"--Provided by publisher.
 Includes bibliographical references and index.
 ISBN 978-1-60014-500-1 (hardcover : alk. paper)
 1. Ghosts--Juvenile literature. I. Title.
 BF1461.S87 2010
 133.1--dc22   2010011398

This edition first published in 2011 by Bellwether Media, Inc.

Printed in the United States of America, North Mankato, MN.

080110   1162

CONTENTS

CHAPTER 1
SOMETHING STRANGE ABOARD

QUEEN · MA

The RMS *Queen Mary* seemed like an ordinary ocean liner. It sailed the seas from 1936 to 1967. It was **beached** in California and became a museum and hotel. However, many people have noticed something strange about this ship. Noises ring through the halls. People see odd shapes. Many people believe that the ship is **haunted**.

RMS *Queen Mary*

A young girl named Jackie once drowned in the ship's pool. People say her ghost still splashes in the water. Some visitors hear the screams of men and the sound of crushing metal. Others hear the cries of children when no children are present. The ghost of the captain reportedly roams the ship.

People have taken blurry photographs of the ghosts aboard the *Queen Mary*. Ghost experts have studied the ship. No solid **evidence** of ghosts has been found. Are the ghosts real, or are they just imagined?

ECHOES OF THE CURACOA?

The *Queen Mary* once collided with a British Navy cruiser called the HMS *Curacoa*. The crash split the *Curacoa* in half and killed many men. Some people think the screaming sounds come from the ghosts of these men.

HMS *Curacoa*

CHAPTER 2
WHAT ARE GHOSTS?

Those who believe in ghosts think that ghosts are the spirits of people who have died. They believe the spirits stay in this world. The spirits may not know how to leave or may have chosen to stay. **Skeptics** believe that ghosts do not exist. They search for evidence to prove all hauntings can be explained.

People have reported many types of ghosts. An **apparition** is a ghost that appears in human form. A **fetch** is the visible spirit of a person who is still alive. A **poltergeist** is a ghost that moves objects. The word *poltergeist* is German for "noisy ghost."

Many people believe ghosts haunt graveyards. Ghost researchers consider St. Louis Cemetery #1 in New Orleans, Louisiana to be the most haunted graveyard in the world.

GRAVEYARD GHOSTS

GETTYSBURG GHOSTS

In 1863, American Civil War soldiers fought the bloody Battle of Gettysburg. Over 51,000 soldiers died in just three days. Some people believe the ghosts of the dead soldiers haunt the battlefield, fighting the battle again every day!

Some people believe ghosts are confused spirits. They think ghosts do not know how to move on from this world. Many ghosts are thought to be the angry spirits of murder victims. Most ghosts seem to stay near the place where they died and appear to family members. Battlefields are often thought to be haunted. There are many places for researchers to search when they look for evidence.

THE CIHUATETEO

The ancient Aztecs believed that women who died in childbirth returned as ghosts called *Cihuateteo*. These ghosts were said to wander the streets stealing children.

Types of Ghosts

Apparition — A ghost in the shape of a human, but without flesh

Atmospheric — A ghost that appears in only one place and repeats the same action over and over

Demon — An ancient, powerful, and evil spirit

Fetch — The visible spirit of a living person

Phantom — A ghost that looks like a living, breathing human being

Poltergeist — A ghost that moves objects

FAMOUS GHOSTS

Ghost	Place
The Bell Witch	Tennessee
Borley Rectory	England
The Brown Lady	England
The Amityville Horror	New York
The *Queen Mary*	California
Abraham Lincoln	Washington, D.C.
Gettysburg	Pennsylvania
The Chase Vault	Barbados

Event

In 1817, a ghost haunts the Bell family, making noises and even pulling blankets off of beds.

A poltergeist said to be the spirit of a dead nun haunts Borley Rectory.

The Brown Lady haunts a country house called Raynham Hall; in 1936, a photographer takes a famous photo of the ghost on the building's stairs.

Ghosts are said to haunt a house in the town of Amityville; the ghosts reportedly drive a man to kill his entire family in 1974; the family that moves in after the deaths leaves after only a few months, claiming the house is haunted.

Several ghosts, including the ghost of a girl who drowned in a pool, are said to haunt a beached ocean liner named the *Queen Mary.*

The spirit of former President Abraham Lincoln apparently roams the halls of the White House.

The ghosts of dead soldiers are said to haunt the Civil War battlefield of Gettysburg.

Ghosts are blamed for moving coffins in the Chase family vault.

CHAPTER 3
SEARCHING FOR ANSWERS

thermal camera

It is hard to prove that ghosts exist. **Ghost hunters** look for clues. They try to record the whispers of ghosts. Special cameras search dark places for ghostly shapes. Ghost hunters often measure the temperature in a room. Sudden drops in temperature may come from ghosts. A **thermal camera** can help hunters locate the ghosts. Hunters also sometimes hold a **séance**. They believe this ceremony allows them to communicate with ghosts and other spirits.

Skeptics try to prove that ghosts do not exist. They go to supposedly haunted places and look for other explanations. Strange sounds might be old pipes or squeaky floorboards. A cold chill might come from a drafty window. A ghostly photo may be a **hoax**. Photographers have used tricks to make it look like their pictures are of ghosts. Experts can detect these tricks.

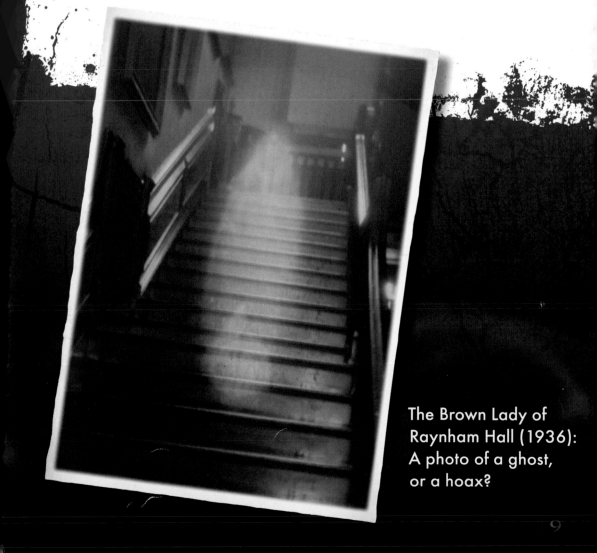

The Brown Lady of Raynham Hall (1936): A photo of a ghost, or a hoax?

GHOST WHISPERS

The recorded sounds of ghosts are called electronic voice phenomena (EVP). Ghost hunters believe that some audio recording devices can capture ghost sounds that human ears cannot hear.

The idea of ghosts has been around for thousands of years. Many people from around the world have claimed to see ghosts. Could all of these people be wrong, or are the spirits of the dead really among us?

GLOSSARY

apparition—a ghost in the shape of a human, but without flesh

beached—run onto land

evidence—physical proof of something

fetch—the visible spirit of a living person

ghost hunters—people who look for evidence of ghosts

haunted—describes a space where a ghost or spirit lingers and makes its presence known

hoax—an attempt to trick people into believing something

poltergeist—a ghost that moves objects

séance—a ceremony through which some people believe spirits of the dead can be contacted

skeptics—people who do not believe in something

thermal camera—a camera that detects and shows differences in temperature; ghost hunters use thermal cameras to detect ghosts.

TO LEARN MORE

AT THE LIBRARY

Brucken, Kelli M. *Ghosts*. Farmington Hills, Mich.: KidHaven Press, 2006.

DeMolay, Jack. *Ghosts in Amityville: The Haunted House*. New York, N.Y.: PowerKids Press, 2007.

Stone, Adam. *Haunted Houses*. Minneapolis, Minn.: Bellwether Media, 2011.

ON THE WEB

Learning more about ghosts is as easy as 1, 2, 3.

1. Go to www.factsurfer.com.

2. Enter "ghosts" into the search box.

3. Click the "Surf" button and you will see a list of related Web sites.

With factsurfer.com, finding more information is just a click away.

INDEX

The images in this book are reproduced through the courtesy of: Jon
Eppard, front cover, pp. 8-9, 10-11, 12-13, 14; Pat Eyre/Alamy, pp.
4-5; Dale O'Dell/Alamy, pp. 6, 20-21; Getty Images, p. 7; Peter D., p.
18; Ulrich Mueller, p. 18; Time & Life Pictures/Getty Images, p. 19.